THE *quilting* MANUAL

Featuring 16 quilt experts!

Techniques, Troubleshooting & More

• Designs for Hand & Machine •

stash BOOKS.

an imprint of C&T Publishing

Text, photography, and artwork copyright © 2017 by C&T Publishing, Inc.

PUBLISHER: Amy Marson

CREATIVE DIRECTOR: Gailen Runge

PROJECT EDITOR: Alice Mace Nakanishi

COMPILER: Lindsay Conner

DEVELOPMENTAL EDITORS: Liz Aneloski, Cynthia Bix, Stacy Chamness, Lynn Koolish, S. Michele Fry, Deb Rowden, and Kesel Wilson

TECHNICAL EDITORS: Carolyn Aune, Stacy Chamness, Mary E. Flynn, Georgie Gerl, Ann Haley, Ellen Pahl, Sandy Peterson, Amanda Siegfried, Teresa Stroin, and Sadhana Wray

COVER/BOOK DESIGNER: April Mostek

PRODUCTION COORDINATOR: Zinnia Heinzmann

ILLUSTRATORS: Mary E. Flynn, Valyrie Friedman, Laura Lee Fritz, Geta Grama, Tim Manibusan, Cheryl Malkowski, Wendy Mathson, Kirstie L. Pettersen, Jessica Schick, Aliza Shalit, Richard Sheppard, and Hari Walner

PHOTOGRAPHY by Diane Pedersen, Christina Carty-Francis, Luke Mulks, and Sharon Risedorph, unless otherwise noted

COVER PHOTOGRAPHY by Lucy Glover

Published by Stash Books, an imprint of C&T Publishing, Inc., P.O. Box 1456, Lafayette, CA 94549

Library of Congress Cataloging-in-Publication Data

Names: C & T Publishing.

Title: The quilting manual : techniques, troubleshooting & more - designs for hand & machine.

Description: Lafayette, CA : Stash Books, 2017.

Identifiers: LCCN 2016034851 | ISBN 9781617455360 (soft cover)

Subjects: LCSH: Machine quilting--Handbooks, manuals, etc.

Classification: LCC TT835 .Q5448 2017 | DDC 746.46--dc23

LC record available at https://lccn.loc.gov/2016034851

Printed in the USA

10 9 8 7 6 5 4 3 2 1

CONTENTS

by Christine Maraccini

THE BASICS of MACHINE QUILTING

Throughout my quilting career I have quilted on both a domestic (tabletop) and a longarm machine. I'd like to take a moment to debunk the myth that a longarm machine is a magical tool that produces amazing quilting. A longarm quilting machine does make machine quilting more convenient and efficient. However, it is not necessary to use a longarm machine to achieve beautiful quilting. Everything in this book can be done on either a domestic or a longarm machine. The quality of the quilting is dependent on you and your ability to freehand draw the designs that you choose to quilt, not on the technology of the machine that you are using.

tips for free-motion quilting on a domestic machine

Quilting Feet

For free-motion quilting you will need a free-motion or darning foot for your machine. My favorite ones have a clear ring or oval that presses against the fabric as you sew. These are great because they enable you to see where you are going. Usually the circle on the bottom of the foot has a relatively accurate measurement of 1/4˝ in radius, which can come in handy as a spacer when you are echo quilting. Each brand of sewing machine has specific feet that will fit on it. See your local sewing machine dealer to get the correct foot for your personal machine.

Each brand of machine has its own quilting feet. I prefer the type with a clear ring or oval.

Your Working Style and Your Work Space

One of the biggest complaints about machine quilting is the difficulty of maneuvering a large quilt under the short arm of a domestic sewing machine. My working style is to quilt in continuous paths whenever possible. This enables me to roll the quilt so that just the path I need is exposed. I can start at one end of the quilt and sew one design, non-stop, until I reach the other end of the quilt. I hate to start and stop, so I try to do it as little as possible. Remember, our goal is to get these quilts finished!

Your workstation can be either fancy or simple as long as it has a flat surface behind and to the left of your sewing machine large enough to hold the weight of your entire quilt as you sew. I quilt at my kitchen table with my sewing machine located at the front right corner of the table.

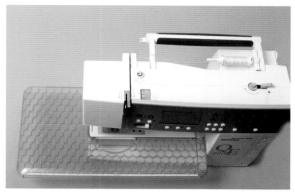

Your workstation can be simple or fancy. I prefer simple, so a large table and a machine with a nice extended base are perfect.

When I have an especially large quilt I add another table to the back of my kitchen table to increase the surface area. I also like to use an extended base on my sewing machine when I'm quilting. This extra surface allows me to maintain better control over the area I'm quilting.

TIP····▶ *If your quilt seems to be sticking to the extended base, wipe the base with a small amount of Pledge cleaner and the surface will become slicker. As you would after contact with any chemical, be sure to wash your quilt when completed to remove any residue.*

tips for free-motion quilting on a longarm machine

The most commonly used longarm machines in the industry have the following things in common: a large throat, long canvas leaders to pin your quilt layers to, and a smooth carriage system to move the machine while you sew. I prefer to "float" my quilt tops on my longarm machine. This means that I pin the backing fabric onto the leaders. I then lay the layer of batting onto the backing near the top leader and then lay the quilt top onto the batting. I pin the quilt top through the batting and onto the backing. I allow the quilt top to drape over the front edge of the machine. This allows me to adjust the quilt top as I work. I can fix any spots that are uneven or have extra fullness as I move down the quilt.

The most important thing I can tell you about using a longarm is that it takes practice. These are not magic machines. The general rule is that it takes one full year to become comfortable and proficient on a longarm. You will get better each time you finish a quilt. Ask your local quilt guild if they have charity quilt tops that need to be quilted. This is a great opportunity to get in some extra practice. Also, take lessons from experienced teachers who are familiar with the brand of machine you use. Be sure to take a maintenance class for your machine as well. Take time to learn how your machine operates in the specific climate and conditions that it is in. Because a longarm has so many moving parts and tension dials, you need to practice and experience how your machine works in order to truly get the most from this wonderful piece of equipment.

starting and stopping

How to start and stop, that is the question! I'm not happy if my starts and stops are visible. In fact, most quilt show judges are not happy to see these either. Whether on a longarm or a domestic machine, I use a method that involves what I've been told is a hand-quilting knot. Always start quilting in a spot that's easy to hide, such as a seam or the base of a leaf or flower. When starting, I drop the needle and raise it so that I can pull the bobbin thread to the top of the quilt.

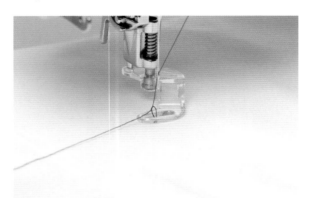

Pull the bobbin thread to the top.

I hang onto the two tails (bobbin and needle threads), then drop the needle back into the exact same hole that I pulled the bobbin thread through earlier. Hang on tight to the tails so that you don't get a nest of thread on the back of your quilt! Start sewing from that point. Once you have laid down a few inches of stitching, it's safe to let go of the tails and tie them off. Tie a square knot (left over right, then right over left), landing the knot exactly over the hole that your stitching started at. Pop the threads through a self-threading needle.

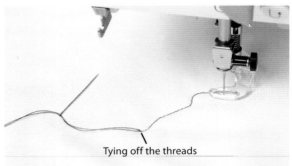

Tying off the threads

Slide that needle under the top layer of your quilt, starting at the hole where you began sewing, and proceed in the direction of your quilting.

Pull the needle out an inch or two away from where you began. Give the needle a little tug and the square knot will pop into the hole where you began sewing. Clip these threads close to the top of the quilt and the thread will disappear. When you run out of thread in your bobbin or spool, or stop quilting, use the same process. If you don't have long enough tails of thread, unsew back to a good junction (the base of a leaf, a seamline, and such), and then pull the bobbin thread to the top and continue from there.

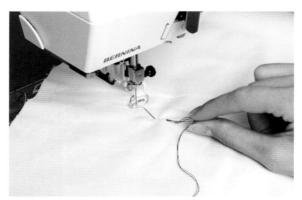

Burying the knot

THREAD *and* FABRIC

by Christine Maraccini

the role of thread, needles, and fabric

Traditional quilting has often neglected the artistic element that thread can add to a quilt. It seems like many quilters thought that beige was the only color of thread on the market. Worse yet, many quilters used that clear stuff so that they could hide their quilting. Although these threads have their place, I say it's time to revolt! There are many new types of thread on the market, and it's time we show off our quilting and use some of them. Break out the bright variegated threads or test that metallic thread you've been intimidated by. You work hard to make your topstitching designs pretty, so make sure they can be seen.

Don't forget the thread! This is the final artistic element that you get to add to your masterpiece.

If you own a sewing machine it is important to know and understand the basic principles of thread and needles, and their relationship with fabric.

Friction and Thread Breakage

The top thread goes through the needle and fabric several times before it finally gets to stay there. The friction of the fabric scraping the thread can break it. Even if it doesn't break, it can be shredded, which means that your quilting is weak and might not stand the test of time. For this reason use a large needle with a deep groove. The large needle will punch a larger hole in the fabric, reducing the amount of friction from the thread passing through the hole. The deep groove also protects the thread by sheltering it from the rough edges of the hole. My needle of choice for general quilting is an 80/12 topstitch sharp or metallic needle. Don't worry about the large holes left in the fabric; these will close up with washing or they can be steamed closed.

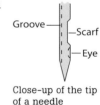

Groove — —Scarf —Eye

Close-up of the tip of a needle

Another thing to consider is the type of thread you are using and whether you are sewing on a domestic or longarm machine. Different threads have varying strengths and thicknesses, which must be considered when choosing the appropriate needle. To make your decision easier, I've included a handy reference chart to guide you in the needle selection process.

General Needle Guidelines for Various Threads

Thread type	Domestic machine needle	Longarm machine needle	Reason
Standard-size cotton and matte polyester (looks like cotton)	Topstitch 80/12 sharp	Sharp 18 (MR 4.0)	Requires a medium- to large-diameter needle
Shiny polyester (looks like silk) and dissolvable	Topstitch 90/14 sharp or metallic	Sharp 16 (MR 3.5)	Requires a smaller-diameter needle
Extra-thick cotton and metallic	Topstitch 90/14 sharp or metallic	Sharp 19 (MR 4.5)	Requires a larger needle

Tension

When you change the thickness of the thread, the top tension needs to be adjusted to compensate. If you have been piecing with a standard thread and change to a thick thread, the tension discs need to be loosened to accommodate the thicker thread. Not only will the thicker thread cause a tension increase, but the tension discs will also flatten the thread. Flattened thread has a tendency to shred since it doesn't move through the needle properly.

TIP···▶ *When your tension is off, the rule of thumb is this: Too much top thread showing on the back of the quilt = tighten your top thread (higher tension number). Too much bobbin thread showing on the top of the quilt = loosen your top thread (lower tension number).*

On a domestic machine, a low tension number equals looser tension. A high tension number equals tighter tension.

Luckily, you will seldom need to change the tension on the bobbin thread on a domestic machine. Try adjusting the top tension first. If the bobbin thread is stronger than the top thread, it will cause your top thread to break; however, it's perfectly okay if the bobbin thread is not as strong as the top thread. Unless you're sewing with metallic thread, it's usually okay to use the same thread in the bobbin as you are using in the top. When using metallic in the top, use silk-style polyester in the bobbin.

Many factors affect the tension in a longarm machine. The general rules for thread and tension mentioned above apply to a longarm as well as a domestic machine. Refer to the reference guides for your particular brand and model for the finer details. Always test the tension prior to quilting, even if you haven't changed threads. Factors such as temperature and humidity can affect the thread and the many moving parts of your machine. My favorite trick is to take all that leftover batting I have lying around and cut it into small squares the size of my hand. I have a basket of these next to my machine and I use them to test my thread tension and clean any oil residue from the needle prior to quilting.

· ·

unraveling the mystery of fancy thread

The Value of Quality

The most important thing to keep in mind when considering fancy thread is to get the good stuff. *It's worth your time and money to purchase quality thread.* You will encounter less breakage and your finished product will be more durable. It has taken a tremendous amount of time and energy to make your quilt; it would be foolish to save a couple of dollars on an inferior thread for the quilting. Second-rate threads have a greater tendency to break and shred while you quilt with them. The time you save with less breakage will surely pay the cost of higher-quality thread.

Cotton Threads

Cotton threads come in solid and variegated colors as well as a variety of thicknesses. A good-quality cotton thread is made of long- or extra-long-staple cotton. The staple is the length of the cotton fiber used to make the thread. The longer the staple, the fewer the lengths of fiber twisted together. This means greater strength and less lint. When using 100% cotton threads I prefer extra-long-staple Egyptian cotton or high-quality long-staple cotton. If the label on the end of the spool doesn't give you the staple length, you can assume that it is short-staple cotton and is an inferior thread. Never use glazed cotton for machine quilting; it can gum up your tension discs, the needle, and the bobbin works of your machine.

Synthetic Threads

My other favorite threads are made of polyester or a blend of polyester and cotton. I avoid rayon threads, which have a reputation for being weak, becoming brittle over time, not being heat resistant, and not being colorfast. Polyester threads can be made with a matte finish to look and act like cotton threads and produce little or no lint. Polyester threads also come in a shiny finish to look like silk. Because of its strength, polyester can be made in many different thicknesses to fit different uses. The thinnest polyester threads are terrific for trapunto work.

Metallic Threads

Metallic thread is intimidating to many quilters. When used sparingly, metallic thread can add that extra oomph that your quilt needs. When choosing a metallic thread, look for a thread with a nylon core and an outer protective surface. Test metallic thread for suppleness. It should drape and move like a standard thread does. If you pull some off the spool and it maintains its coil, put it back on the shelf and move on. I use Superior brand metallic threads with a lot of success.

I use a 90/14 metallic needle for metallic threads. This type of needle has an extra-deep groove to protect the thread. Drop the top tension all the way down to 1 or 2 on a standard sewing machine and begin test sewing. Slowly bring the tension up until you find what works best for your machine. Write down the tension so that you won't have to go through this process again. When using metallic thread in the top, fill your bobbin with a good-quality silk-style polyester thread.

TIP ···▶ *I like to write the tension setting directly on the spool end so that I know where to find it next time.*

NOTE

Fiction: *100% cotton thread is the only thread that is safe to use on a cotton quilt. Synthetic thread can "cut" the fibers of your quilt fabric.*

Fact: *It's perfectly okay to use modern threads made of synthetic materials. In order to prevent the thread from cutting the fabric, the fabric and thread need to be similar in strength. The good-quality threads on the market have been manufactured and tested to be safe in your quilts.*

fabric

The first step toward fantastic machine quilting is to start with good-quality fabric. Some fabrics are more abrasive than others. Many of the inexpensive bargain fabrics on the market are the biggest problem. I'm sure there is a good explanation for why this is so; I've just had too many bad experiences with these types of fabrics to waste my energy on them. The money you save will not be worth it when you try to quilt and your thread keeps breaking. Do yourself a favor, and piece your quilts with good-quality, supple fabrics. When you are ready to quilt them, you will be able to focus on the designs instead of spending your time trying to figure out why your thread is breaking again and again.

by Alex Anderson

CHOOSING QUILTING DESIGNS

Traditional and innovative quilts have several things in common when you are considering which quilting designs to use. The guidelines generally hold true for both, and are also applicable to both machine and hand quilting. When I am deciding how to quilt my tops, I always keep the guidelines in mind. However, as we all know, guidelines are subject to interpretation. Each quilt top needs to be considered individually. This makes the entire quilting journey an interesting and challenging experience from conception to conclusion.

guidelines

Will intricate quilting designs show? Not all quilts are candidates for awesome quilting designs. It is a sad day when you have spent the time stitching incredible quilted motifs only to find that they are lost in the pattern of the fabric. If a quilt is destined for fabulous quilting, make sure that the fabric you use is plain enough to let the quilting designs show.

While planning the quilt, designate areas that will be highlighted with quilting. Solid-colored fabrics are your best bet for those areas, or a printed fabric that reads almost as a solid will work. If you are at all unsure, test the quilting on the fabric to see if it shows.

If your border fabric is highly patterned and fancy quilting isn't going to show, I have two solutions that work quite well.

1. Follow the printed fabric design to create your quilting design. When using this technique, make sure that there is an even density of quilting.

2. Fans and cables are another nice solution. They are repetitive, so the brain can easily identify what the pattern is.

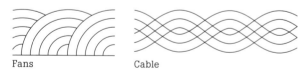

Fans   Cable

Fan design on printed fabric

Sometimes just by changing the thread color used for quilting, the design will become more prominent.

Quilting with white thread

Quilting with pink thread

Many times new quilters are taught to quilt ¼″ from the sewn line. I believe this is so the quilter does not have to decide what to quilt and can simply get her hands going. The problem is that this technique can lead to some areas being heavily quilted while other areas are left without enough quilting.

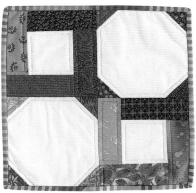

¼″ quilting

Fill the space. Remember when you were in kindergarten and your teacher would constantly remind you to fill the space? The same holds true when deciding what designs to quilt. A design that is too small looks awkward and empty. If you are filling a specific area, for example an alternate solid-color block, end the design about ¼″ from the sewn line. In addition to filling the space, this will help avoid quilting through the seam allowances.

Not adequately filling the space

Use an equal amount of quilting over the entire surface. If one area is tightly quilted and another area is left empty, not only will the quilt look odd, but it will not lie flat or hang straight.

Be careful not to over quilt, especially when machine quilting. The quilt might become stiff.

Use an adequate amount of quilting. Even the simplest quilt deserves due respect. Always read the batting manufacturer's recommended quilting density for the specific batting you are working with. Also follow the manufacturer's instructions for proper preparation for use.

Uneven amount of quilting

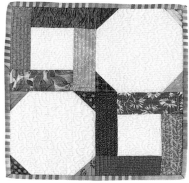

Too much quilting

Adequate amount of quilting

It's okay, and in fact perfectly fine, to cross over seamlines of pieced units. Look how much more interesting it is to have a crosshatch grid crossing over pieced seamlines than ¼˝ quilting would have been. Also, a border consisting of several units (inner borders and a main border) can be quilted with one motif.

It is nice to mix geometric lines with soft, curved lines. That is why you will often see gridded backgrounds used with fancy motifs. They work well together and act as complements. The gridded background accentuates the fancy designs. Make sure the density of the grid is in proportion to the size and scale of the design.

Before you start to design your quilting designs you must determine if your quilt is going to be quilted by hand or by machine. If you are designing for hand quilting, anything goes. If machine work is in the quilt's future, consider how many stop/starts you are creating.

Motif with no background quilting

Motif with grid quilting

BLOCK SKELETONS

by Gina Perkes

I like to refer to this design technique as "skeletons" because it begins with a very basic shape that will later be enhanced and customized. This technique is perfect for lovers of freehand quilting because minimal marking is required. Just one basic block skeleton can easily become a collection of very different block motifs.

template plastic

I keep about ten sheets of thick, transparent template plastic in my stash of necessary supplies and tools. Template plastic is invaluable for use in many different applications. Because it is transparent, it can be positioned either directly over the actual fabric block or over a drawn paper block for sizing. Once you've sketched a design skeleton that you like on the plastic, cut it out using nonfabric scissors. The plastic shape can be traced repeatedly and then set aside for future use. I frequently refer to my collection of saved templates for new projects.

Place the transparent template plastic directly over either your presectioned quilt block or pre-sectioned paper block. Draw a very basic shape on the plastic and cut it out.

Trace the template directly onto the quilt, using an erasable pen, or onto the paper block. Mirror-image the template to complete the quadrants.

If you'd like to begin your own collection, create a template using this basic block skeleton design. You can enlarge or reduce it to accommodate any block size. Mirror-image the template to complete a quadrant.

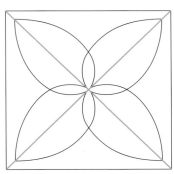

Basic, symmetrical block skeleton

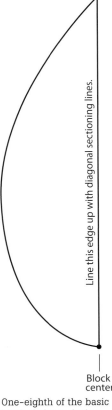

Line this edge up with diagonal sectioning lines.

Block center

One-eighth of the basic block skeleton design

Now you have a completed block skeleton that is waiting to be embellished with freehand details. Vary the details added based on the style of the quilt. You can further change the outcome of the motif by adding details to different portions of the skeleton (inner edge, outer edge, both edges). A variety of different block designs can result from the same basic skeleton. By varying the placement and style of the freehand details, you can create a collection of very different motifs.

TOOLS *for* MARKING QUILTING DESIGNS

by Alex Anderson
and Angela Walters

The following tools have become staples for drawing quilting designs. Many of these tools are available at your local quilt shop or fabric store. If not, check out your local art or drafting supply store. Stored with care, they will last you a lifetime.

Pencil, Sharpener, and Eraser

It all starts here. Any pencil will do (mechanical or standard). You just need one with a nice sharp tip (an electric or battery sharpener is very nice to keep handy). Don't be afraid of the pencil. It will soon become your best friend. Remember that it has two ends: the lead and the eraser. Always keep in mind that no design is set in stone until the stitches are laid in place, and even then, changes are possible.

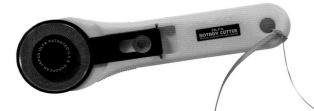

Paper Scissors and Rotary Cutter

A good pair of sharp paper scissors is handy to have. The rotary cutter I use for paper has an old blade that is less-than-perfect for fabric. Both are marked with a tied ribbon to distinguish them from my fabric scissors and rotary cutter.

Black Permanent Felt-Tip Pen

I purchase these by the box. After the quilting designs are established, I go over the pencil lines with a fine-tip marker (such as a Sharpie Fine Point Permanent Marker, *not* the Ultra Fine Point).

Paper

There are many different types of paper available that will work quite well, each offering its own benefits and limitations.

17″ × 22″ graph paper (4 or 8 grids per inch): Graph paper is typically available by individual sheet and by the pad. It is more economical to purchase a pad. The light grid lines make drawing the pattern within the desired space very easy. In addition, the grid increments are helpful to keep the pattern evenly spaced when dividing up the areas of the quilt to be quilted. When the space you are designing for is larger than the sheet of paper, tape the appropriate number of sheets of paper together with clear tape. In addition, gridded paper is resistant to multiple erasures.

Velum on a roll: Velum is a heavy-duty tracing paper. It is translucent, yet strong enough to withstand multiple erasures. This is a nice feature when you are faced with drafting patterns. It comes in varying widths on a roll (18″ or wider). Velum is expensive, so look to your pocketbook and purchase the widest roll you can afford.

Tracing paper on a roll: Tracing paper is much less expensive than velum and is also translucent. However, it is not as sturdy as velum and will not hold up to multiple erasures. Again, look to your pocket book and purchase the widest roll you can afford.

White butcher paper on a roll: This very economical paper is what I use for patterns. It is not translucent, but it is tough and will stand up to multiple erasures.

Most of these papers are also available by the sheet or pad. If necessary, you can purchase extra-large tablets of the paper you want to work with. The advantages of a roll of paper are that you can easily draw borders, and purchasing by the roll is more economical. In all cases, if the design you are working on exceeds the size of the paper, you can piece it together with clear tape.

Compass

This handy tool comes in a variety of styles, prices, and quality. The kind of compass used in grade school is perfectly fine for small to medium circles. The only problem is that sometimes they slip and refuse to hold true to a size. A more expensive compass is nice to work with and will hold the size. Make sure it comes with an extension arm for drawing larger circles. For really large circles, there is a tool made especially for yardsticks. This gives you the ability to draw circles up to 72″!

Protractor

Any protractor will work quite nicely. It is important that you understand exactly where the 0° line is: some protractors have it on the edge, and some have it set in ¼″ or so.

Light Table

A light table provides a light source that will enable you to trace your paper pattern onto the quilt top. Any flat, clear surface with light shining through will work. It can be as simple as a window. My light table is an 18″ × 36″ piece of ¼″-thick, clear Plexiglas. When it is time to draw, I set it between two chairs and put a lamp under it. If you have a dining room table that extends with leaves, consider getting the Plexiglas cut a couple inches larger than the size of your leaves. Extend your table but do not put the leaves in. Place the Plexiglas over the opening and place a lamp under it. Your table will surround the "lightbox." Of course, a commercial lightbox will also work, but I prefer having a larger surface to work on.

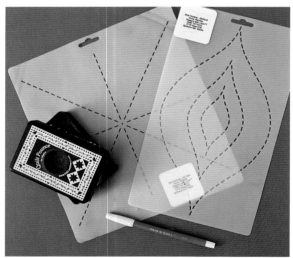

A variety of marking tools will make quilting easier.

Water-Soluble Pens

I will admit that I am a snob when it comes to water-soluble pens. I use only Dritz blue marking pens. I have never had a problem with the marks not coming out, so I figure, why try anything else? I am very cautious to remove the marks quickly, using only cold water, following the manufacturer's instructions.

Chalk

Chalk is a great way to mark dark fabrics or quilts that I don't want to get wet. Chalk pencils and chalk sticks are great for this purpose.

Stencils

Stencils are great for quickly marking designs on a quilt. The stencils I use most often are grids for marking registration lines. The registration lines help me keep my designs even. I use a chalk pounce pad to mark the stencils. The pad holds blue or white chalk and can be rubbed over the stencil to quickly mark the design. Stencils are available in all different shapes and sizes.

TIP ···▶ *When choosing stencils, make sure they are continuous line or machine-quilting stencils. Hand-quilting stencils have too many starts and stops and will be frustrating.*

Rulers

If you are quilting on a longarm quilting machine, make sure you have a good-quality ruler. I use a 2″ × 12″ acrylic ruler. It is great for marking lines and for guiding the machine along straight lines and seams.

Notions

Don't forget the little things such as pins, scissors, and extra needles.

additional supplies for domestic sewing machines

Quilting Gloves

Quilting gloves help you grip your quilt and maneuver it through your domestic sewing machine (DSM). This will help you focus more on your quilting and less on wrestling with the quilt.

TIP···▶ *Quilting gloves are great for longarm quilters, too. They allow you to hold on to your rulers and templates securely without cramping your hands.*

Supreme Sliders

One of the biggest complaints of quilting on a DSM is the drag of the quilt on the machine. Pushing and tugging your quilt can leave you worn out and ready to call it quits. The Supreme Slider is a Teflon sheet that lies on the bed of the sewing machine and allows the quilt to slide through the machine with less friction. Most machine quilters wouldn't consider quilting without one of these handy tools.

Free-Motion Foot

When machine quilting with your DSM, you will need a presser foot made especially for free-motion machine quilting. This type of presser foot (sometimes called a darning foot) allows you to see your quilting area and disengage the feed dogs, and it will make your quilting experience even better.

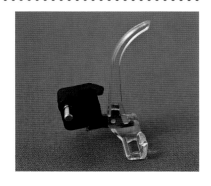

TENSION *and* HAND PLACEMENT

by Don Linn

tension

It is very important to have proper tension when machine quilting. If the bobbin thread tension is too loose or the top thread tension is too tight, the bobbin thread will tend to be pulled to the top of the quilt, and the top thread will lie flat against the quilt top. Conversely, if the bobbin tension is too tight or the top thread tension is too loose, the bobbin thread will lie flat against the back of the quilt, and the top thread will be pulled to the bottom.

Good tension

Top tension too loose or bobbin tension too tight

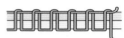

Top tension too tight or bobbin tension too loose

Threads are made from different materials and come in different diameters. These variables affect how the thread flows off the bobbin, and this ultimately has an effect on tension and stitch quality.

top or spool tension

This is one place the tension can be adjusted on machines with standard bobbin cases. It is the only place tension can be easily adjusted on machines with a drop-in bobbin.

Many machines have a knob on the front of the machine to adjust tension.

NOTE

To adjust the tension, just remember this old saying "lefty-loosey and righty-tighty."

Most of the new electronic machines have a menu that will allow you to adjust the tension by tapping the screen. If you have a menu to tap, generally the higher the number, the tighter the tension will be.

Bobbin Tension

A good starting point for bobbin tension is doing what is called the yo-yo test. To do this, remove your bobbin and case from the machine and, with the bobbin still in the case, hold the thread between your thumb and forefinger. Dangle the bobbin case in the air and gently bounce it up and down. If the bobbin and case fall to the ground, the tension is too loose.

If they do not drop at all, the tension is too tight. The case should drop just slightly each time you bounce it.

The bobbin also uses the "lefty-loosey and righty-tighty" adjustment method.

This is just a starting point, and further adjustments may have to be made as you check your actual stitch quality.

Yo-yo test

Stitch Quality

One of the biggest challenges in machine quilting is maintaining a good stitch quality.

Problem

The bobbin thread lies flat on the back, or the top thread is visible on the back in the form of dots at the beginning and end of each stitch.

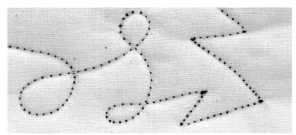

Top tension is too loose; back of quilt.

SOLUTION

Increase the top tension or reduce the bobbin tension and retest.

Use a larger-diameter needle.

CAUTION

If you increase the tension too much, you will see the top thread lying flat against the fabric. This is kind of like walking a tightrope, so make your adjustments in small increments.

Problem

The top thread lies flat on the top, or the bobbin thread is visible on the top in the form of dots at the beginning and end of each stitch.

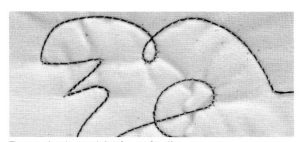

Top tension is too tight; front of quilt.

SOLUTION

Decrease the top tension or increase the bobbin tension.

Use a larger needle.

CAUTION

If you adjust the tension too much, you will see the bobbin thread lying flat on the back.

hand placement

Hand placement is very important when machine quilting. I like to think of my hands as an embroidery hoop that moves the quilt sandwich through the machine.

TIP···▶ *In fact, it is possible to put the sandwich in a hoop or lay a hoop on top of the quilt and then hold onto it as you move the quilt sandwich.*

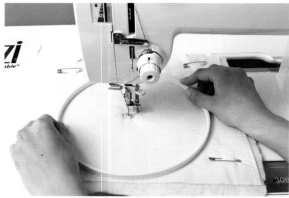

Using embroidery hoop

If you place your hands on both sides of the needle, you will have much better control than if you place your hands at the edge of the extension table.

Good hand placement

Adjust the position of your hands depending on which direction you will be stitching. If you know that you are going to be stitching from left to right, for example, when you start stitching, place your right hand as close to the needle as possible, leaving extra space between your left hand and the needle. This will give you a larger range of motion. Keep in mind that you are going to be starting and stopping many times, so the farther you can go between times when you have to move your hands, the more efficient you will be in the long run.

PLANNING *the* QUILTING ACROSS *the* QUILT TOP

by Christina Cameli

Facing a big quilt can be a little daunting. Go in with a plan.

I usually break up the quilt into rough sections and decide on an order for quilting them. I choose the sections based on the size of the quilt and the design I want to stitch. I start with the center areas whenever possible. This allows any fullness of the quilt to be pushed outward as I go, making puckers less likely. I also appreciate finishing the hardest part while I am fresh and full of energy. It's all downhill from there! I work in a counterclockwise direction around the quilt's perimeter when I can, which aids in visibility.

5	4	3
6	1	2
7	8	9

16	15	14	13
5	4	3	12
6	1	2	11
7	8	9	10

If I'm stitching a directional design such as stretchy meandering, I generally work in large columns or rows. Again, I start with the center column and work outward.

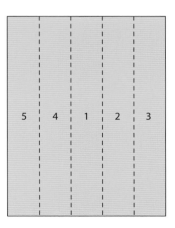

| 5 | 4 | 1 | 2 | 3 |

by Christina Cameli

CREATING REGULARLY SPACED DESIGNS

Use a guide to help you with stitching a regular design. The guide can be marks made with a fabric marker or pencil, pins placed at regular intervals (place them so you can stitch around them when possible), or my favorite, a piece of painter's masking tape.

Mark a piece of tape at the intervals where you want the design to repeat. Place it on the quilt top, making sure it is straight and level. Use the marks on the tape as landmarks for the repeating design, being careful not to stitch into the tape itself. Reposition this piece of tape with each new row, or as needed.

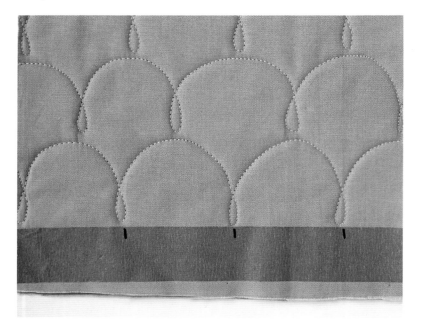

TIP···▶ *You can use a piece of tape, unmarked, to keep a linear design straight and level across a quilt top.*

by Christina Cameli

ENVISIONING *the* QUILTING PATTERN

It can be difficult to envision a quilting design on a quilt. If you need to see it before you commit, try one of these tactics.

Take a digital photo of the quilt (or a portion of the quilt) and print it out on regular printer paper. Sketch the design you are envisioning over the picture. Print a few copies to compare different quilting designs.

For a technology-free option, lay a piece of clear vinyl over a portion of the quilt top. (Quilter's Vinyl from C&T Publishing works well for this.) Sketch the quilting design on the vinyl with an erasable marker. Be very sure to keep the marker away from the edges and avoid smudging the ink onto your hands or the quilt.

Sketching quilting design on picture of quilt top

by Hari Walner

BACKGROUND STITCHES

Backgrounds are stitched in areas directly next to quilting designs you want to showcase. They give the impression of receding behind a motif, much as a sky is in the background of a landscape painting. Some quilters call these stitches "fills."

a good background

Good background stitching adds texture and richness to your quilt without detracting from the featured quilting design. This texture is created by the quilting lines being closer to each other than the lines in the main quilting design.

Background quilting can appear a bit darker than the quilted design, even when the same thread is used for the design and the background. This is because lines of stitching create ditches when the quilt layers are compressed. The ditches create shadows. Background quilting has many lines of stitches close to each other, so more shadows are created. This slightly darker, textural effect is a lovely design element.

Photo by Dennis Dolan

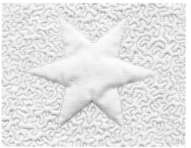

Density makes a difference.

what works

When deciding how close to stitch the lines of quilting in your background, consider how large or complex the quilted designs are. Make your background quilting dense enough so your quilting design will stand out.

The goal is not to make these lines of background stitches as close to each other as possible, but to space them so they best show off your quilted designs. Very small motifs need closer background stitching to increase the contrast. Larger motifs do not need the same density.

It often helps to experiment on a small sample piece with a portion of the quilting design to see how tightly you want to stitch the background. If your stitches are too widely spaced for the design, you miss an opportunity to accent the design.

by Angela Walters

QUILTING NEGATIVE SPACE

The negative space, or the background, of a quilt is my favorite part of the quilt. The designs you use in this area can expertly enhance and transform your quilt into something exciting! In this section, I share some of my favorite quilting designs to use in the negative space of a quilt.

Since the negative space of a quilt can be any shape or size, I use the term "quilting area" to represent it. The quilting area can be anything from the block background to the whole quilt.

decide how much you want the quilting to show

I almost always use thread that blends in with the quilt top; I don't want the quilting to take away from the quilt! The examples in this section are quilted with a contrasting thread color so that the stitches will show up in the photographs. You may have noticed that modern quilters tend to match the thread color to the fabric, but this is your design decision!

try using the designs in different ways

The designs in this section need not be relegated to the background only! Most of them would be great allover designs or can be adapted to fit into larger blocks or borders.

play around

You don't have to quilt the designs exactly how I show you—give them your own twist.

*by Hari Walner and
Christina Cameli*

FREE-MOTION QUILTING
tips

1. When you have extra quilt bulk in your machine because of a large project, try to fold the quilt in deep pinch pleats rather than rolling it. A rolled quilt can be cumbersome and tiresome to handle. Office binder clips are great for holding the pleats together.

2. Gather enough of the quilt around the needle so that you only have to move the area of the quilt that you are stitching on. The quilt should be flexible enough so the weight of your hands resting on the quilt will easily guide it under the needle. If you spread the quilt out flat on your sewing table, you will have to move the whole quilt every time you take a stitch.

3. Never watch your needle while you are stitching. Instead, watch the line of the design that you are feeding into your needle. Looking ⅛″–¼″ down the road will help you stay in control.

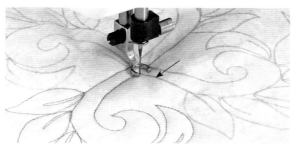

4. Relax and remember to breathe while you are stitching. Holding your breath from anxiety will not help your quilting—your brain and your muscles need the oxygen.

5. Use a fresh, sharp needle.

6. Warm up on a practice pad.

7. Stop worrying; start stitching.

8. Keep breathing.

9. Look ahead of the needle.

10. Let your shoulders and elbows relax.

11. See what happens if you stitch a little faster.

12. If you feel out of control, stop, breathe, and then start again.

13. Don't be afraid to experiment.

14. Keep practicing; you're getting better every time!

by Christina Cameli

TROUBLESHOOTING

When the machine suddenly sounds or feels different as you stitch, stop and check the back of your work to make sure you aren't missing a problem. Nothing is more disheartening than having to spend an entire hour ripping out a few minutes of stitching.

When you get the sensation that the quilt is starting to catch at the corners of the machine, or becoming harder to move, *stop*. Adjust the quilt so that it can move freely around the machine. Fluff out the corners to keep them from binding. You'll probably need to do this frequently when stitching a large allover design.

should you rip it out?

No one's quilting is perfect. So when the quilting doesn't go as you expect, should you take out the offending stitches and try again or just keep on stitching?

If you have a tension disaster, definitely take out the stitches and redo them. Loose loops of thread will not hold up over time. For the more common occurrence, where the tension is fine but the stitching just didn't go where it should have, decide whether it's a Big Mistake or a Little Inconsistency.

Big Mistakes draw attention to themselves. Nonquilters can point them out. You can find them immediately even after stepping away from the quilt top for a bit. They hurt to look at. Go ahead and take these out so they stop tormenting you.

Little Inconsistencies blend in to the overall pattern on the quilt top. You stitched a wonky spiral or a wobbly leaf? The meandering crossed its own path? You stitched into a corner and had to stop and start over again somewhere else? These things happen to everyone. Nonquilters don't notice them, and even you may have to search to find them again later. Leave these Little Inconsistencies in. You will get better from stitching, not from taking out stitches. Take all the time you just saved by leaving those stitches in, and go stitch something else!

avoid these mistakes

In the hopes that you can avoid some mistakes, here's a list of frustrating things I've done to myself.

Stitching the corner of the quilt to itself: When you are stitching near the edges of the quilt, make sure you can see the edges and corners of the backing fabric so you know they are not folded beneath the area you are working on. You may want to bring each corner of the backing fabric around to the top of the batting and hold it in place with a basting pin to make it less likely that the backing can be turned under as you work.

Stitching the edge of the quilt to the darning foot: If you stitch off the edge of the quilt top, come back onto it slowly, making sure the darning foot goes over rather than under the quilt top. If you do happen to stitch the quilt top over the darning foot, remove the darning foot from the machine, remove the quilt, and then rip out the stitches from the back.

Stitching so close to a pin that it can't be removed: It's tempting to stitch right up against a pin instead of removing it. But it's inconvenient to find the darning foot trapped against a pin you stitched too close to. When this happens, break the thread, remove the pin, and restart the stitching. Make sure to remove any pin from the stitching area, or at least those within an inch or two of where you are stitching.

POTENTIAL PROBLEMS

by Don Linn

I am commonly asked what the proper stitch length is. Unfortunately, I can't give you a definitive answer to this question. You are the artist, and you should strive to have a stitch length that is pleasing to you. I will tell you that I like to have my stitches close to the same length as my machine's default stitch, which I use for piecing.

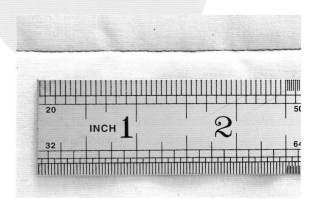

Correct stitch length

Concentrate on making your stitches a consistent length all the time. If you can make them all pretty close to the same length, then I can tell you what you need to do to get them to the length that pleases you.

Problem

A very common problem students face when they begin machine quilting is that their stitches are too short.

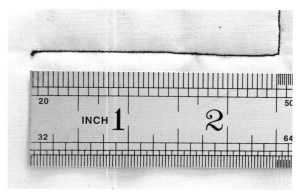

Stitches too short

CAUSE

Moving your hands too slowly in relation to the speed of the needle going up and down causes small stitches.

SOLUTION

To lengthen your stitches, you have two variables you can adjust. You can either speed up your hands or slow the speed of the needle. All too often, when I tell my students to slow the needle speed, they slow both the speed of their hands and the speed of the needle. This does not lead to any change in the stitch length, because they have changed both variables at the same time. It is almost as if their hands are connected to their feet; move one, and the other follows suit. You must change only one variable at a time to notice any change in the stitch length.

Concentrate on finding a hand speed that you are comfortable with. You should easily figure this out after a very short amount of time spent practicing.

Problem

Having stitches that are too long is another common problem.

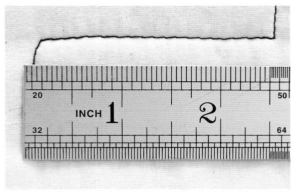

Stitches too long

Moving your hands too fast in relation to the speed of the needle going up and down causes large stitches.

SOLUTION

To shorten the stitch length, you have the same two variables to adjust as when the stitches were too short. You can get your stitches shorter by either slowing your hands down or making the needle go up and down faster. Do not adjust both variables at the same time. Use the table below as a quick guide to adjust stitch length.

Problem

Rounded points or V's of designs

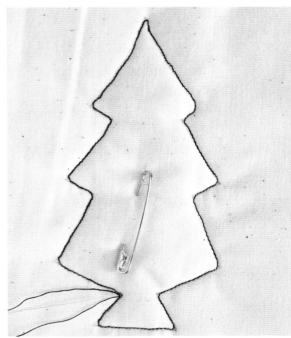

Rounded points or V's

POSSIBLE CAUSE

If you are stitching a design with sharp points or V's, like a star, you may notice that sometimes they are rounded or chopped off. Even though you are following the design exactly, what is probably happening is that as you approach the point or V, the needle is beginning its upward cycle. When the quilt is moved to where the needle will intersect the point or V, the needle is still coming up or just beginning to go down. By the time the needle pierces the fabric, you have moved beyond the point or V and have started down the other side of the design. This causes the chopped-off or rounded look.

SOLUTION

When you come to the sharp change in direction, pause at the point or V and take 2 stitches. That way you can be assured of having a nice, crisp design. Once again, say to yourself, "Stitch, stitch" at the point or V. The 2 stitches in one place will not be at all noticeable. As you get more proficient with your stitching, you will probably be able to cut this down to one stitch, but you must stay alert and not get lazy.

HAND QUILTING

by Sylvia Pippen

traditional and contemporary sashiko

Sashiko, which means "little stabs" in Japanese, is a simple running stitch traditionally used to work intricate designs with white thread on indigo fabric. Sashiko has been a compelling and practical art form for centuries and was originally used to strengthen and sandwich layers of cloth for warmth in northern Japan.

Traditional Sashiko designs abound. Kamon, or family crests, and natural objects, such as cherry blossoms or cranes, are stylized into dozens of variations. Geometric designs, all with ancient historical meanings, are also well suited to Sashiko.

Pine

Today Sashiko has evolved from a practical art form into decorative surface embellishment, with the thread pulled through only the top layer, rather than through all three layers, of a quilt sandwich. Sashiko can stand alone or dramatically complement pieced or appliqué quilts. The beauty of Sashiko is its simplicity: A humble running stitch can outline the most intricate design. I use traditional Japanese geometrics and Kamon crests in my quilts but am continually discovering new twists to this old art form.

Lightning

Seven treasures

Hemp leaf

Bamboo

Although Sashiko lines can be stitched by machine, the machine's continuous stitching line does not give the soft look of hand Sashiko, in which stitches have space between them that allows the background to show. If you are a machine quilter, I encourage you to try hand Sashiko. You might be surprised at how fast it goes and how calming it is to sit down and stitch a beautiful Sashiko design.

sashiko hand quilting supplies

Sashiko requires very few supplies beyond a sharp needle with a big eye, thread, scissors, suitable fabric, and perhaps a sturdy thimble. No hoop is required. Your Sashiko project is easy to carry along and can be done anywhere, even in less-than-optimal light.

Sashiko Thread

Japanese Sashiko thread is made of loosely twisted, long-staple cotton. This type of cotton is very strong and comes in many colors and in fine, medium, and thick weights. Perle cotton #8 and #5, embroidery floss, crochet thread, and silk are alternative threads. Experiment to find what works best for your project.

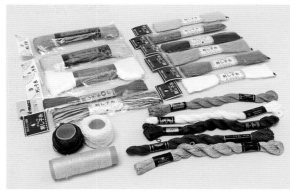

Sashiko threads

Needles

The right Sashiko needle will make your stitching enjoyable and will eliminate wear and tear on your hands. Unlike quilting thread, Sashiko thread is thick and bulky, so the needle has to pierce a hole in the fabric large enough to easily pull through two thicknesses of thread and the eye of the needle. Sashiko needles are very sharp, thick, and strong and come in different lengths and thicknesses. Experiment with different size needles and types of fabric. If one needle is too hard to pull, try another size. Alternatively, you can use embroidery or crewel needles.

It is also important to choose a needle with the right thickness and length for your project. For tightly woven fabrics, use shorter and smaller needles. For looser-weave fabrics, use longer needles so you can gather more stitches at a time. Thimbles are optional.

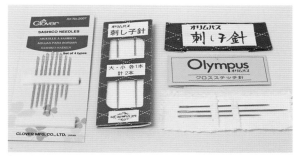

Sashiko needles

Fabrics for Sashiko

Sashiko was traditionally stitched on hand-dyed indigo cotton, linen, hemp, or other plant fibers. Don't use true indigo dyed fabric if you are going to combine it with appliqué, as the indigo may bleed when washed. Some reproduction indigos and sturdy commercial cottons are dye-fast. Avoid using batiks, as the thread count is too fine for Sashiko.

Fabrics for Sashiko and appliqué backgrounds

marking the design

The easiest way to mark Sashiko designs on dark fabric is to use a waxless, white transfer paper. Be sure to test your transfer paper first to make sure it produces a clean line and does not smear. Mark carefully—not all transfer paper markings will wash out.

1. Place the transfer paper with the white side down on top of the fabric. Position the pattern on top of the transfer paper.

2. Pin on one side of the pattern, through all 3 layers, and mark part of a pattern line using a stylus, a fine lead pencil, or a ballpoint pen. Open on the pin hinge to make sure the line is transferring well. The hinge allows you to check your line without disturbing the pattern's placement.

3. Pin all 4 corners outside the design. Trace and transfer the design.

If a Sashiko design has a simple shape or curve, trace the shape onto template plastic or card stock. Then cut out the shape and use a chalk pencil to trace around the pattern onto dark fabric.

Geometric designs with straight lines can be transferred using a ruler and transfer paper or by marking a grid on the fabric with a chalk pencil.

THREAD TIP ··▶ *Sashiko thread pulls more smoothly and tangles less if you thread it in the needle so that you are pulling with the twist instead of against it as you stitch.*

To test the twist, hold up a single thread, pinch close to the top of the thread between your thumb and forefinger, and run your fingers down the length of the thread. It will feel rough one way and smooth the other. You want it to feel smooth when you run your fingers down the thread. Tie a colored thread at the top of the thread bundle when it is positioned correctly, and always pull your threads and thread your needle from this end.

stitching a sashiko design

1. Either pull a thread from your traditional Sashiko thread bundle or cut a 20″–24″ length of perle cotton or other thread. Thread this through the large eye of a sharp needle and make a single knot at the end.

2. Bring the threaded needle up from the back of the marked background fabric. You may start stitching at any point along the design, but do plan a stitching route that does not require too many twists, turns, or long skipped spaces on the back.

3. Place the point of the needle flat on the design line a short distance from the point at which the thread emerges; measure this distance. This will help you gauge how long the stitches should be before you pull the needle through the fabric. If the needle is angled or held straight up before taking a stitch, the point may not stay on line or you may misjudge the stitch length.

STITCHING TIP ···▶ *In Japanese sewing, the needle is held still and the fabric placed on it in a pleating action. Put some light tension on the fabric and rock it, gathering several stitches onto the needle.*

4. Take 2–3 stitches onto the needle. Keep the length of the stitch the same (5–7 stitches per inch). Traditionally, the stitch on top is slightly longer than the space in between. However, evenness is more important than stitch length.

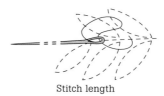

Stitch length

5. Pull the needle and thread through to the knot.

6. After stitching an inch or two, pull up on the thread a little. Using your thumb, carefully stretch out the stitching. The idea is to keep the work loose, especially the thread on the back, so the fabric does not pucker.

IRONING TIP ···▶ *Always iron your finished work from the back so the Sashiko stitching isn't crushed or made shiny.*

by Laura Lee Fritz

START QUILTING

Practice your machine quilting in order to find your rhythm, and learn to sew at a constant speed.

TIP···▶ *Warm up by tracing the designs with your fingertips or a pencil to practice the paths. This tracing makes the pattern a physical memory and helps you quilt more smoothly. You may even learn to stitch many of them freehand.*

sewing a continuous-line quilting design

Note any pattern sections where you change sewing direction, sew over an area twice, or sew over an existing line of stitching. You may find it helpful to draw arrows using a highlighter marker on the pattern to guide you.

For most of the patterns the starting and stopping points are indicated. You can start at either end of the pattern and sew left to right or right to left.

When you start or end a line of quilting, or when your top thread or bobbin is depleted, knot the end(s) of your stitching line and thread a needle with the thread tails. Use a long-eye sharp embroidery needle for the tail so both threads will fit through at once. Try wrapping the pair of threads around the eye tightly, pinch the thread to hold the tiny loops as you withdraw the needle, then slip the eye over these tight little loops. Sew these ends by sliding the needle back along your quilting line, pull the needle out, bury the knot into the batting, and cut the tail.

QUILTING DESIGNS: *motifs*

Designs by Natalia Bonner

Designs by Geta Grama

Designs by Geta Grama

Designs by Geta Grama

Designs by Jenny Carr Kinney

Designs by Jenny Carr Kinney

Designs by Jenny Carr Kinney

Designs by Don Linn

Designs by Don Linn

Designs by Don Linn

Designs by Don Linn

Designs by Cheryl Malkowski

Designs by Gina Perkes

Designs by Gina Perkes

Design by Gina Perkes

Designs by Sylvia Pippen

Design by Kathy Sandbach

Designs by Kathy Sandbach

Designs by Kathy Sandbach

Designs by Kathy Sandbach

Designs by Kathy Sandbach

Designs by Jessica Schick

Designs by Jessica Schick

Designs by Hari Walner

QUILTING DESIGNS:
borders

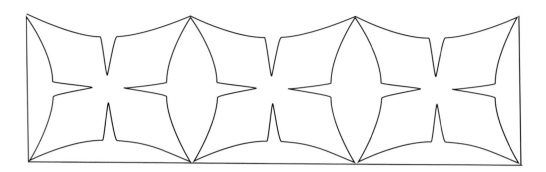

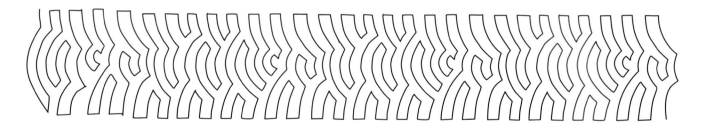

Designs by Laura Lee Fritz

Designs by Christine Maraccini

Start

Designs by Christine Maraccini

Designs by Sylvia Pippen

Designs by Sheila Sinclair Snyder

Designs by Sheila Sinclair Snyder

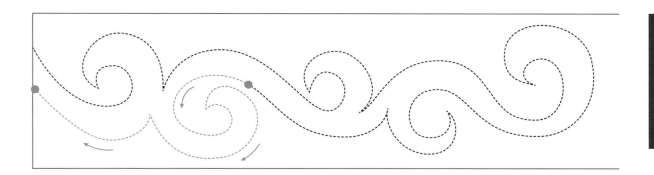

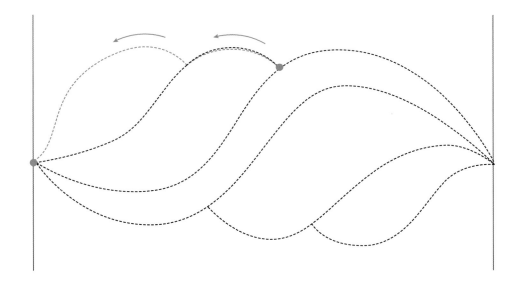

Designs by Angela Walters

QUILTING DESIGNS:
allover

Designs by Christina Cameli

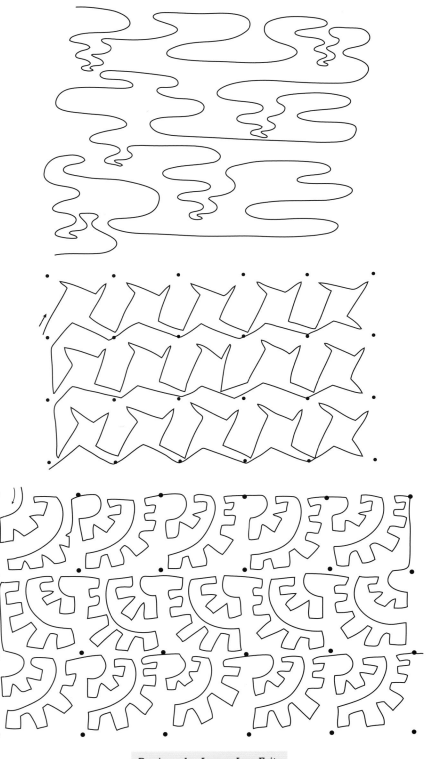

Designs by Laura Lee Fritz

Designs by Laura Lee Fritz

Designs by Cheryl Malkowski

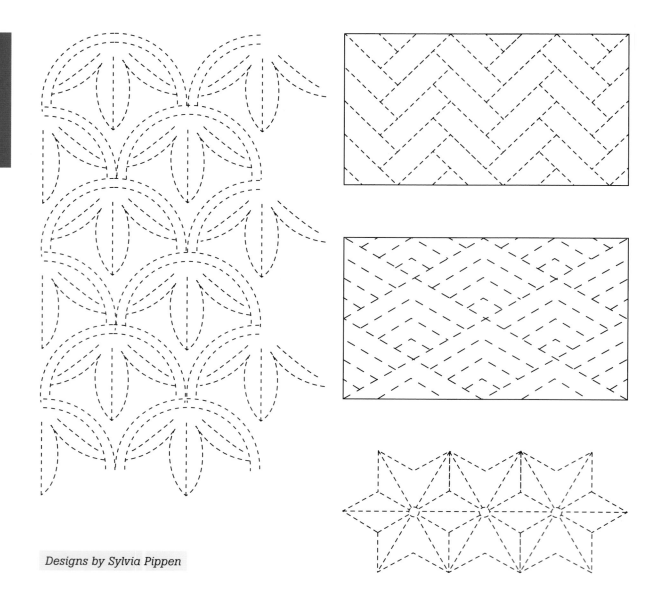

Designs by Sylvia Pippen

TIP ···▶ *These allover designs are perfect for hand quilting.*

Designs by Sheila Sinclair Snyder

Designs by Sheila Sinclair Snyder

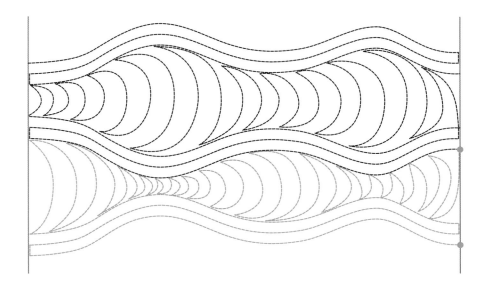

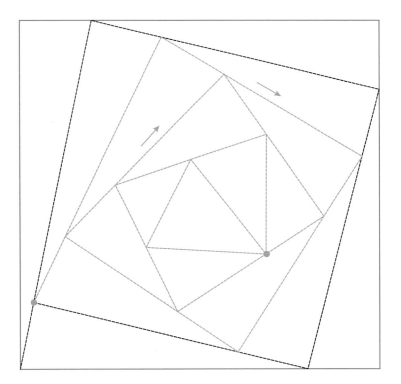

Designs by Angela Walters

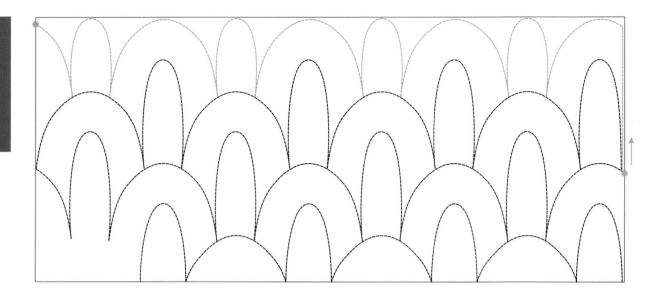

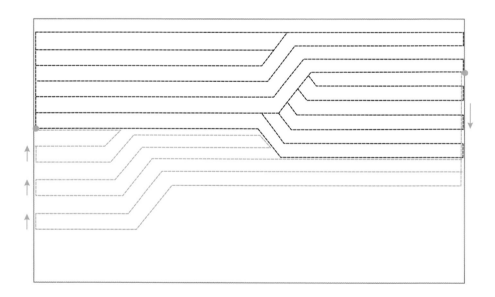

Designs by Angela Walters

Designs by Natalia Bonner

Designs by Natalia Bonner

ABOUT *the* DESIGNERS

Alex Anderson

seeks to educate, entertain, and grow today's quilting community. Longtime host of the television show *Simply Quilts*, she is also an executive producer and cohost of *The Quilt Show* with Ricky Tims. Alex lives in Northern California. **alexandersonquilts.com**

Natalia Bonner

has been quilting professionally for many years. She is a teacher, pattern designer, and popular blogger with numerous awards for her work. Natalia lives in St. George, Utah. **piecenquilt.com**

Christina Cameli

is a nurse, midwife, and quilter who enjoys finishing quilts on her domestic machine in addition to teaching free-motion quilting classes for beginners. She lives with her husband and children in Portland, Oregon. **afewscraps.com**

See more of Alex's quilting designs in *Beautifully Quilted with Alex Anderson*, available from C&T Publishing.

See more of Natalia's quilting designs in *Beginner's Guide to Free-Motion Quilting* and *Next Steps in Machine Quilting— Free-Motion & Walking-Foot Designs* by Natalia Bonner, available from Stash Books.

See more of Christina's quilting designs in *First Steps to Free-Motion Quilting* by Christina Cameli, available from Stash Books.

Laura Lee Fritz

is widely known for her hand appliqué quilts and her fanciful wholecloth quilting, filled with narrative images from the stories surrounding her life. Laura raises bluetick coonhounds and Navajo-Icelandic sheep in rural Sonoma County, California, but steps off of the farm to teach quilting classes nationwide. **lauraleefritz.net**

Geta Grama

discovered quilting, absolutely by chance, on the Internet. Seduced by the new world of combining fabrics, colors, and patterns, she abandoned her engineering profession and devoted her time entirely to quilting. Geta lives in Romania. **getasquiltingstudio.com**

Jenny Carr Kinney

has been making quilts since 1968 and professionally teaching for more than 30 years. She specializes in historically inspired antique reproductions and period-appropriate quilting motifs sewn with modern equipment and using today's techniques. Jenny lives in Ventura, California.

See more of Laura's quilting designs in *Mindful Meandering* and *250 New Continuous-Line Quilting Designs* by Laura Lee Fritz, available from C&T Publishing.

See more of Geta's quilting designs in *Shadow Trapunto Quilts* by Geta Grama, available from C&T Publishing.

See more of Jenny's quilting designs in *Quilting Designs from the Past* by Jenny Carr Kinney, available from C&T Publishing.

Don Linn

started his journey in quilting with a longarm machine and not a clue how to operate it. He has learned a lot since then and is now a well-known teacher of piecing and machine quilting. Don lives in Redding, California.

Cheryl Malkowski

has been quilting since 1993 and loves all aspects of quilting, except the handwork. She started designing quilts in 1998 for her pattern company, Cheryl Rose Creations. Cheryl lives in Roseburg, Oregon. **cherylmalkowski.com**

Christine Maraccini

began a successful machine-quilting business in 2000 in order to stay home and raise her children. Since then she has received various awards and helped create a quilt for ABC's *Extreme Makeover: Home Edition*. Christine lives in Nevada. **christinescustomquilts.weebly.com**

See more of Don's quilting designs in *Free-Motion Machine Quilting* by Don Linn, available from C&T Publishing.

See more of Cheryl's quilting designs in *Doodle Quilting* by Cheryl Malkowski, available from C&T Publishing.

See more of Christine's quilting designs in *Machine Quilting Solutions* by Christine Maraccini, available from C&T Publishing.

Gina Perkes

owns and operates a quilting training facility and Innova longarm dealership, The Copper Needle. The recipient of numerous awards, Gina travels to guilds and conferences teaching her techniques on domestic and longarm machines. She lives in Payson, Arizona.

thecopperneedle.com

Sylvia Pippen

grew up in the San Francisco Bay Area and was taught to sew at a very early age by her mother. Sylvia specializes in Japanese sashiko and appliqué quilt designs. She now resides in La Conner, Washington.

sylvia-pippen.com

Kathy Sandbach

began quilting in 1982 when she attended a quilting class with a friend. First as a hobby, and then as a means of extra income, Kathy began to machine quilt full-time. Kathy passed away in June 2012 and will continue to be missed by all who knew her.

Jessica Schick

discovered longarm quilting and quickly built a full-time business around it, quilting 300 to 350 quilts each year. She creates patterns for quilting, embroidery, and other crafts through her company, Digi-Tech Designs. She lives in Wisconsin.

digitechpatterns.com

See more of Gina's quilting designs in *Mastering the Art of Longarm Quilting* by Gina Perkes, available from C&T Publishing.

See more of Sylvia's quilting designs in *Paradise Stitched— Sashiko & Appliqué Quilts* by Sylvia Pippen, available from C&T Publishing.

See more of Kathy's quilting designs in *Show Me How to Plan My Quilting* by Kathy Sandbach, available from C&T Publishing.

See more of Jessica's quilting designs in *Quilting by Design* by Jessica Schick, available from C&T Publishing.

Sheila Sinclair Snyder

is not afraid to step away from traditional thinking. She backs it all up with a solid foundation from her many years of teaching, sewing, and writing patterns and books. Sheila lives in Eugene, Oregon. **licensetoquilt.com**

Hari Walner

has been teaching quilting since the 1990s, with an emphasis on free-motion machine quilting, trapunto effects, and the creative use of threads. *The Professional Quilter* named her as their 2006 Teacher of the Year. Hari lives in Colorado. **hariwalner.com**

Angela Walters

is a machine quilter who loves to teach others to use quilting to bring out the best in their quilt tops. Her work has been published in numerous magazines and books. She shares tips and finished quilts on her blog and believes that "quilting is the funnest part!" Angela lives in Kansas City, Missouri. **quiltingismytherapy.com**

See more of Sheila's quilting designs in *Get Addicted to Free-Motion Quilting* by Sheila Sinclair Snyder, available from C&T Publishing.

See more of Hari's quilting designs in *Hari Walner's Continuous-Line Quilting Designs*, available from C&T Publishing.

See more of Angela's quilting designs in *Free-Motion Quilting with Angela Walters* and *Shape-by-Shape Free-Motion Quilting with Angela Walters*, available from Stash Books.

Want even more creative content?

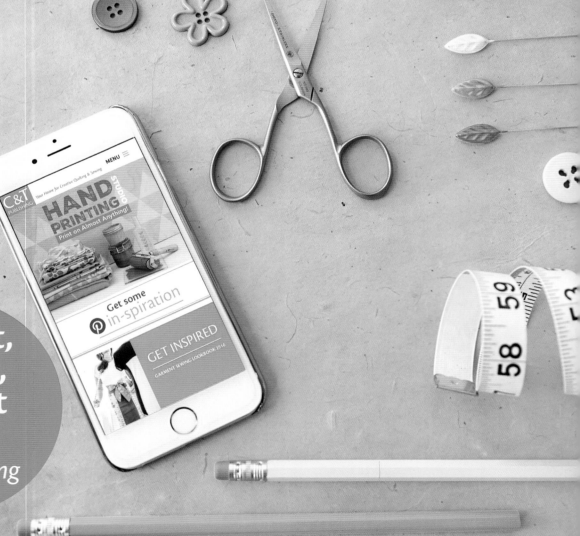

Make it, snap it, share it *using* #ctpublishing